Change in Accounts Payable

AP Now Speed Learning Series

Mary Schaeffer

Parts of this book may have previously appeared in
other books written by Mary Schaeffer, the Accounts
Payable, the Accounts Payable Now & Tomorrow
monthly newsletter, on the AP Now YouTube
podcast and in various talks given by Mary Schaeffer.
Bulk purchases can be arranged by contacting the
author.
ISBN 978-1-7351000-8-1

ABOUT THE AP NOW SPEED LEARNING SERIES

AP Now Speed Learning Series is a series of short books all designed to be read in 60 minutes. They focus on timely issues relevant to the accounts payable and payment function. They are intended for the busy professionals who work in, manage and/or have responsibility for the accounts payable and or payment function.

Change in Accounts Payable

CONTENTS

Introduction

In today's fast-paced and dynamic business environment, the only constant is change. Nowhere is this truer than in the realm of finance and accounting, and more specifically, accounts payable. Traditional processes and practices are rapidly evolving by advances in technology, automation, new and ever-innovative frauds, evolving regulations, and shifting market dynamics. One area that stands at the forefront of this evolution is the accounts payable function. As the financial heart of an organization, accounts payable plays a pivotal role in managing cash flow, vendor relationships, avoiding fraud, and financial stability.

The significance of accounts payable cannot be overstated. It serves as the intersection where financial commitments are met, supplier partnerships are nurtured, regulatory reporting is managed and financial data is processed. Yet, the function of accounts payable is undergoing a profound metamorphosis, changing forever the fundamental structure of the process by which financial obligations are met. The old manual processes are fast giving way to automation and digitization. Regulatory bodies are intensifying their scrutiny, necessitating additional and more sophisticated compliance.

Tomorrow's accounts payable department will look very different from today's. The very basic processes are changing, invoices are no longer largely paper, payments are no longer largely being made by paper checks and sadly, fraud is evolving at a rate faster than anything else.

Planning for a future that allows the organization to compete requires some very basic changes. This quick read book is designed to start you on that transformative journey, one towards a future where accounts payable becomes a strategic partner rather than a mere transactional function.

Chapter 1:
The Accounts Payable Department

In last five to ten years the responsibilities of the accounts payable team have evolved and were expanding slowly. The process was jumpstarted with the advent of COVID and many organizations taking their accounts payable remote, almost overnight. And for those who were not able to go remote, the whole experience served as a wakeup call to move away from paper.

Very quickly, the function is evolving away from one focused primarily on accurate data entry to one requiring top-notch management, analytical and executive skillsets. Many of these expansions involve tasks that were just not traditionally done. They are as a result of either expanded regulatory reporting requirements or expanded best practices to help the organization thwart off potential fraud. Let's take a look at some of the changes.

New Responsibilities in Accounts Payable

- **Change #1:** Vendor set-up has gotten a lot more complicated on two fronts: fraud prevention and regulatory compliance. requires lots more effort and analytical skills. Vendor validations are just the start. They have gotten a lot more complicated as criminals become a lot more enterprising and regulatory authorities more accurate.

New Tasks: It is no longer acceptable to just set a vendor up using information on an invoice. that may be the starting point. But, validating as many of those pieces of information as possible is now a best practice.

Also, it is important to continually monitor changes made to vendor files to ensure neither your employees, nor your vendors' employees nor crooks are playing games with the data.

New Skills: Employees must understand OFAC, FCPA and other regulatory requirements impacting every organization. The fines and reputational damage to the organization can be severe, if these requirements are not adhered to.

- **Change #2:** Verify change of bank account and rush wire requests from high level executives. As most reading this are probably aware, there has be an onslaught of fraud attempts using both phony change of bank account requests and Rush wire requests. These are usually a result of some sort of email manipulation or an attempt to trick an employee using a very similar URL. While there is a recognition that these tasks must be done, few management teams have taken into consideration just how much time it takes to do some of these verifications.

  New Tasks: Timely verifications of any request that is out of the ordinary

Also, taking the extra minute or two to examine closely the email address associated with a request.

New Skills: Ability to decipher phony email addresses

- **Change #3:** Identify and respond to new frauds and change processes to accommodate needed protection routines. The pace that new frauds swept through the marketplace in the last few years has been nothing short of horrific.

  Anyone who works in, manages or has responsibility for accounts payable now has to be on the lookout for the next new fraud. Once it is identified, hopefully before a company becomes a victim, the organization must change its processes to protect against the fraud. Usually this translates into additional, but very necessary work, for the accounts payable staff.

New Tasks: Constantly be on the lookout for the next new fraud. Once it is identified, the management team must make sure that everyone on the team is updated and educated. Also, whatever protection routines need to be incorporated into current processes should be implemented immediately—not when there is some spare time.

New Skills: Ability to recognize new frauds. This is definitely not simple.

Also, everyone should read as much of the current business intelligence so as to be alerted when another organization identifies a new fraud. Our best protection is shared information and that is part of AP Now's mission.

- **Change #4:** Create new routines for a changed and often hybrid working environments that incorporate strong internal controls. Many organizations have learned in the last year that a) the accounts payable function can be handled remotely—at least partially—and b) the company and/or employees wish to continue in a remote fashion some or all of the time.

New Tasks: Revise practices to accommodate either remote working or hybrid working situations to ensure controls are not weakened and all required responsibilities are covered.

New Skills: Flexibility and adaptability—okay, these are not necessarily new skills, but skills that are now more critical than ever.

- **Change #5:** Adapt to new information reporting forms and oversight (1099). Two things happened in the last two years which will radically impact the importance of issuing timely and accurate 1099s each year. First was the introduction of the 1099-NEC. Virtually every professional I spoke with said this January was a nightmare. This includes those who thought they were fully prepared. I've yet to hear from anyone who said it went smoothly.

And, the IRS has already announced changes to the new form it released last year. But that is not the worst part of it. President Biden has requested an additional $80 billion for IRS enforcements. This includes Information Reporting (1099) audits. Even if he doesn't get the full amount he requested, he is likely to get a good chunk of change. And it makes good sense. The IRS estimates that for every $1 it spends on enforcements, they collect $5. It's almost a no-brainer—at least from the IRS's point of view.

New Tasks: More accurate 1099s. This will be more difficult as most organizations have to split the information formerly reported on the 1099-MISC between the two forms: the 1099-MISC and the 1099-NEC.

New Skills: A full understanding of the two new forms and what goes on which form.

There's a lot of change going on, not just in accounts payable but in the whole business environment. And that is a good thing. Management's reaction to the competence shown by the accounts payable staff has been overwhelming enthusiastic. With the new responsibilities and new management admiration, it's accounts payable's time to shine.

Other Ways Work Is Growing

While it's clear that new responsibilities will increase the workload in accounts payable, the magnitude of work being handled in the department has been growing surreptitiously due to other reasons. There's been a lot of talk about how accounts payable departments are getting smaller, thanks to advances in technology. And, to be fair, these improvements do eliminate some of the manual work in accounts payable. But what no one's talking about are the other factors that are increasing the work needed to be done in accounts payable.

That's the focus of this piece. There are certain best practice changes that have needed to be made in order to either protect against a new fraud or to meet new regulatory reporting requirements that increase the work load. Let's take a look at some of them.

- **Change #1**: Increase in the number of duplicate copies of invoices. With the advent of email and the emailing of invoices, suppliers have discovered it's easy (and costs almost nothing) to email the same invoice to more than one person. So, they have embraced this change in droves.

  Guestimates are that about 20% of all invoices are sent more than once. Some are sent two and three times, and this is all before the due date, not because the original invoice is past due. When this occurs, processors have to sort out the duplicates and make sure they aren't processed. Ideally, this happens at the very beginning of the process. Realistically, these invoices sometimes make it almost to the end of the cycle before someone discovers it is a duplicate.

With the projected 20% of all invoices received as duplicates and if, on average, they get processed half-way through before it is discovered they are a copy, this translates into an increase in work of 10%. If an organization has 10 processors, this means that the workload has increased by one person, without an increase in staff. Near as AP Now can tell, no companies are increasing staff to deal with this headache.

- **Change #2**: Verifying change of bank account requests. As readers are painfully aware, phony change of bank account requests have increased massively and they all need to be verified to guard against that one phony one slipping through. That is why most organizations have adopted the best practice of picking up the phone and verifying every single request for a change of bank account, when paying with ACH.

The issue here is that each of these verifications takes a bit of time. Even if it is only 15 minutes, and sometimes it's a lot longer. Why? Because tracking down the right person to verify the email request can sometimes take quite a bit of time. If there are only one or two requests a month, it is not a huge deal. However, for those organizations receiving ten or twenty or more such requests each month, the time adds up.

Yet it is imperative that each of these be verified. You can verify 100 requests and find them all legitimate. Yet, if you don't verify the 101st request, and that one turns out to be phony, you can end up sending millions of dollars to a criminal.

- **Change #3**: Weeding out fraudulent invoices. This is similar to the issue of duplicate invoices, which technically are not fraudulent. Unfortunately, criminals have gotten quite good at creating phony invoices. The accounts payable staff has to spend time processing it before they identify it as fraudulent. IF they are successful and the invoice is flagged and not paid, that is great and the outcome everyone hopes for.

- But the staff must spend valuable time first processing the fake invoice and then researching to make sure it is not legitimate. Again, this is valuable time that could be spent on legitimate tasks. Of course, no one is suggesting that the staff not do the research. But few companies are recognizing the increase in fraudulent invoices and the impact it has on their staff workload. This is another task that is silently zapping the productivity of the accounts payable staff.

- **Change #4**: Keeping up with the ever-increasing regulatory reporting and compliance issues. As most reading this are painfully aware, each year there are changes to the 1099 Forms. This requires time each fall to get updated on the changes, review any new 1099 Forms, and make sure you are ready for the fun that is known as January.

What's more, in the last few years, various states have started adding their own state 1099 reporting requirements. This is a whole other level of reporting and one that very few are adding staff for. Make sure to check your state website to see if your state has added this requirement.

This is in addition to trying to keep track of the changes to sales and use tax, any sales and use tax holidays that might impact your operations and a myriad of other regulatory issues impacting the accounts payable and payment functions.

- **Change #5**: Finding time to learn new technology and adjusting to new best practices to fight new frauds. To be fair, a lot of the new technology is very user friendly. But that does not mean that there isn't a learning curve for most people. Even when there is an update to an existing software, it takes some time to adjust. Think about the last time you had an Office update.

The amount of new technology being thrown at business professionals is astounding. Teams, Zoom and other video conferencing options are now commonly used. It is expected that professionals will figure out how to use whatever option is being offered. And, that is just the beginning.

When it comes to the accounts payable function, many are automating. While eventually, automation does save time, the important thing to remember is that the time savings doesn't happen overnight. Initially, there may even be a productivity slump as the staff struggles to learn the new technology AND convince suppliers to use it.

This is the elephant in the automation room, if you will. Suppliers are often less enchanted with new automation solutions and reluctant to use them. The accounts payable staff then has to spend time trying to convince them to use it. They also then need to sometimes do extra work when certain vendors don't use the new automation process.

This is on top of adjusting processes to the new automation and adjusting processes to fight the new frauds that continually pop up. Again, most, if not all companies, have not factored these issues into their performance expectations of their accounts payable staff.

Concluding Thoughts

Accounts payable staff continue to get smaller, mainly because management expects certain efficiencies from the software solutions they purchase. While it is true that eventually there will be time savings, it doesn't happen as quickly as anyone would like. And, there are a myriad of other issues eating into the valuable resource called time. Perhaps it is time to increase the staff working on these issues?

Chapter 2:
The Process

When Stephen King wrote "sooner or later everything old is new again," I doubt he was thinking about accounts payable. But he could have been writing about the dreadful problem that has skyrocketed in the last few years: the problem of suppliers sending several copies of the same invoice because email makes it so easy – and cheap! Duplicate copies of invoices can lead to the other dreaded duplicate problem: duplicate payments. As most reading this are probably painfully aware, most vendors do not automatically return duplicate payments and only some of them are good about issuing vendor credits.

Finally, even if you are really, really good at catching the duplicate invoices and not making that second payment, they create a lot of non-value add work. Weeding them out can be a nuisance. The goal of every best-practice accounts payable team should be to eliminate these second (and sometimes third and fourth) copies. What's more, since you probably won't be able to get all your vendors to behave, your procedures should include a process to identify those non-compliers.

An Old Problem Reappears: Action Plan to Eliminate Duplicate Copies of Invoices

Duplicate copies of invoices can lead to the other dreaded duplicate problem: duplicate payments. As most reading this are probably painfully aware, most vendors do not automatically return duplicate payments and only some of them are good about issuing vendor credits.

Finally, even if you are really, really good at catching the duplicate invoices and not making that second payment, they create a lot of non-value add work. Weeding them out can be a nuisance. The goal of every best-practice accounts payable team should be to eliminate these second (and sometimes third and fourth) copies. What's more, since you probably won't be able to get all your vendors to behave, your procedures should include a process to identify those non-compliers.

What follows are ten steps to help you get a handle on the duplicate invoice problem.

- **Step 1:** Make sure you've set up a unique email address for invoices. If you can marry an e-fax facility to an email account, also provide a fax number, even if you are using an invoice automation solution.

- **Step 2:** Provide the information of where to email invoices to all suppliers—as many times as necessary to get them to send them to the correct address.

- **Step 3:** Educate employees outside AP, that invoices should be emailed to your preferred emails address and NOT to them. If they are in doubt and receive an invoice by email, they can forward it to the preferred email address with a note that this may be a duplicate.

- **Step 4:** Anytime a vendor sends an invoice to any place but the preferred email address, make them aware of the preferred email address for receipt of invoices.

- **Step 5:** Discourage paper invoices. Make sure suppliers understand that the sooner you receive an invoice, the sooner you can start processing it for payment. It is in their best interest to either submit an invoice through an automation solution or to the preferred email address.

- **Step 6:** Warn suppliers that if they submit invoices by both mail and email, this will delay payment, as they will automatically go on a list the requires dual verification.

- **Step 7:** Warn suppliers that if they email their invoices to more than one person, this will delay payment, as they will automatically go on a list the requires dual verification.

- **Step 8:** Any time you discover duplicate copies being sent, put that supplier on the list of vendors whose invoices are automatically checked twice.

- **Step 9:** If you discover vendors trying to trick you into paying twice, put them on the list of suppliers whose invoices are double checked.

- **Step 10:** In extreme cases, pick up the phone and call vendors to ask them to stop sending copies of an invoice to more than one person. Again, remind them that this delays, rather than speeds up, payment.

Of course, vendors don't always behave in a way that accounts payable would like. Inevitably, no matter how hard you try and explain the benefits of automation and email, there will be some vendors who persist in mailing invoices. You really can't not accept their invoices. You will need to process them; but they will not be your top priority. If you have a really good process for emailed invoices, simply scan the invoices and email them to the preferred address.

The headache and extra work related to duplicate invoices will continue for the foreseeable future. It is your job not to let it turn into the nightmare of duplicate payments.

Another Old Problem Reappears: A 5 Step Action Plan to Reduce Duplicate Payments

Duplicate payments are surging again. This is due to a variety of issues. This is a real problem because, as most reading this are painfully aware, a huge chunk of vendors don't return those funds unless you prompt them. Some even go so far as to willfully hide them. That's why it's imperative that the professionals responsible for an organization's money take the following steps to ensure this problem doesn't balloon on their watch. The following steps will help and should form the crux of any organization's protection plan against duplicate and erroneous payments.

- **Step 1**: Training. It is imperative that staff members are given adequate and regular training. This might include training when they first start, an annual refresher, and extensive training any time new software or technology is introduced. Also, if there is any change in process, there needs to be some training. Sending out an email with instructions is not sufficient. Finally, employees should feel free to ask as many questions as they need during this training without being made to feel they are stupid.

- **Step 2**: Rigid coding standards for data entry should be included in the policy and procedures manual and given to employees during training. If there was one tactic that will have the greatest impact on diminishing this problem, it is this. There is no excuse for any organization not taking this step. Periodically verify that staffers are still using the coding standard and are not entering data however they see fit. The coding standard, sometime called a naming convention, should be for both invoice data entry and setting up vendors in the master vendor file. It should address every aspect of the data, including things like punctuation, spaces, dashes, leading modifiers and long numbers.

- **Step 3**: Centralized receipt of invoices reduces, but doesn't eliminate, the chance of making a duplicate payment. When suppliers are given one postal address, one fax number and one email address to send invoices, the chances of a duplicate diminish. Lately the problem has been growing as they send the invoice to multiple email addresses. It can also occur when they both mail and email an invoice. Make sure suppliers know where to send their invoices.

- **Step 4**: Conduct regular statement audits to identify open credits and retrieve them. But take it one step further. Research every credit that is due to a duplicate payment to determine what happened and where the weakness is in your process that permitted this duplicate to happen. Once you've done that, review how you can change your processes to close that loophole and reduce the chances of a duplicate happening a second time.

This work can be done by someone on staff or if human availability is lacking, an outside firm can be hired for this purpose. If you do this work yourself, consider hiring an outside firm to look for further duplicates, beyond the open credits. By hiring one that works on a contingency basis, you only pay if they recover funds for you.

- **Step 5**: Regular follow up on those sending multiple copies of invoices. A large part, albeit not the only part, of the duplicate payment problem revolves around the sending of the same invoice to multiple parties. Occasionally, no matter how strong the controls are, a few slip through and get paid twice. Even if that doesn't happen, the accounts payable staff spends a good deal of time weeding out these duplicate copies, time that could be spent on more value-added tasks.

  By identifying the suppliers who are culprits of this practice and calling them, you can get some to stop. Others, no matter how much you ask, will continue with the practice. You should note which suppliers are doing this and make sure to check their invoices closely to ensure a second hasn't slipped through.

Duplicate payments happen to everyone. These are fund that come right off the bottom line and cause your organization to be less profitable that it might otherwise be. To expect that a duplicate payment will never get made is completely unrealistic. But the number should be kept to a bare minimum and every step should be taken to annihilate this headache.

Chapter 3
Payments

For a long time, not much changed in the payment world. Yes, 1099 requirements changed each year and we slowly started making more electronic payments but that was about it. In the last few years, that has all changed. New products, new frauds, new technology have all changed that. Let's take a look at five big trends that are greatly impacting your AP, P2P and payment functions.

Emerging Trends Impacting the Future of Payments

- **Going Paperless**: Most companies understood on some level that paper checks are not the ideal payment tool. They require quite a bit of manual non-value add work and they are expensive, more costly than might appear at first glance. When COVID hit, the pandemic shone the spotlight on just how inefficient they were, especially at those organizations that were not able to get payments made without having someone go into the office.

Clearly, this once again shone the light on the inefficiencies associated with paper checks. Some took the opportunity to aggressively move more of their suppliers to being paid either with a card tool or an ACH. Others turned to their banks to have them print and mail their checks. While AP Now is a big advocate of paying via ACH, we also recognize that it will be some time before most US companies are able to ween themselves off paper checks completely.

- **Automation**: When it comes to the P2P process, companies are automating a lot more than just the invoice processing part of the equation. Today some companies are automating the entire accounts payable process while others are taking it one step further and are automating the entire P2P process. Automation is about a lot more than just invoices.

What's more, the technology and the way it is being programed is getting more user-friendly, is incorporating more functionality and getting more affordable. Expect automation and new technology to continue to play a major role in the accounts payable, P2P and payment functions for the foreseeable future.

- **New Frauds**: Fraud continues to be a major concern, especially as accounts payable teams everywhere are the primary targets for criminals. Data from a recent AFP survey notes that 61% of the targets for BEC frauds are accounts payable professionals with another 14% focused on treasury personnel.

Criminals continue to be innovative

exploiting weaknesses in processes that might not be readily apparent. That is why it is imperative that all professionals continually watch for new frauds and adjust processes to thwart the criminals and safeguard the organization.

This is especially important as new payment vehicles such as cryptocurrency (digital payments) and real time payments (such as Zelle and Venmo) creep into the B2B space. There have already been frauds associated with these types of payments and members need to keep alert as they start to use these payments. Some of the frauds involve more than one type of payment, i.e., presenting a stolen check and then being asked for a refund via Zelle.

- **New Best Practices**: Whether it be to protect against new frauds, adjust for a remote or hybrid work situation or to create efficiencies around the use of new technology or regulatory reporting requirement, best practices are changing.

- **New Payment Tools**: At the same time, pressures to increase limits on Same Day ACH, the emergence of Instant and/or Real Time payment and new card products provided reasonable and even attractive alternatives. Some organizations even dipped their toes into digital payments buying or accepting cryptocurrencies.

  With the recent expansion of Same Day ACH (with limits now raised to $1 million) and the Fed and others looking into Real Time payment products, expect to see much change in this area in the next few years. The other change in this arena is the slow creep of P2P payment mechanisms such as Zelle and Venmo into the B2B payment space. This has been slow to date, but it is happening

  Some organizations are now verbally validating all large transactions. Of course, the definition of large will vary from organization to organization. This is to protect against having inadvertently fallen for a change in bank account fraud.

Other organizations that have previously had all ACH transactions handled outside of accounts payable are having them moved to the accounts payable department. This is to take into account the fact that sometimes when payments are made outside accounts payable, best practices are not used.

For example, purchase orders and receiving documents may not be extinguished until the end of the month instead of simultaneously with the payment is being scheduled, when payments are made outside accounts payable. This always presents a risk of duplicate payment, which expand exponentially as more and more payments are made via ACH.

Impact of Changes

As we look at all the issues impacting the way we handle payments today and what is coming down the pike, it appears that flexibility will be the name of the game moving forward.

As new products continue to emerge, so will new frauds. I hope I'm wrong on the last remark but I'm guessing no one will argue with me on that front. This does not mean that we should ignore the innovations, far from it. Rather as we adopt the new products, change our processes and integrate the new technology into our day-to-day operations, we need to take care and ensure our controls are tight.

Then, when the crooks find a way to manipulate around those controls, adjust quickly so they don't take advantage. There's a lot of innovation on the payment front and the next few years promises to be exciting and profitable for those organizations ready to take it on. What is clear as we review all the changes, is that the way every organization makes payments is changing. Hence, it is a really good idea to have an effective payment strategy.

Creating an Effective Payment Strategy to Maximize AP Efficiency

Most organizations use several payment vehicles to pay their suppliers and other obligations. At the end of this chapter, you can see a sample listing all the possibilities, along with when they are generally used.

Why Have a Strategy

Use of several different payment vehicles has the potential to create issues, specifically duplicate payments. To be clear, we are not advocating that you limit your payments to one single vehicle, just that you be aware of the duplicate issue and address it as you set up your payment strategy.

Without a set strategy, different processors will use a different payment vehicle for the same invoice making it difficult to figure out what went on. When p-cards first became popular in the corporate world there were a plethora of duplicates that resulted from payments being made on the card and by check.

What's more a set strategy means that your suppliers will know what to expect and where to look for your payments. It makes it less likely that you will receive a second copy of the invoice, as cash application will be done faster on their end.

And of course, you need a set strategy so your processors know how to schedule each invoice for payment. Your strategy will allow them to do so your organization has the most effective payment plan, minimizing efforts on their part and keeping costs associated with making payment as low as is feasible.

Sample Strategy

It is important that every organization create a formalized payment strategy so their processors can all schedule payments in the same manner. There is no right or wrong strategy, just a consistent one. What follows is a sample strategy, you might modify to meet your own requirements.

- Use checks as last resort, encourage other types of payment as follows:

- Issue p-cards to frequent purchasers and have them all low-dollar items (say under $2500) with the company card.

- ACH credits used to pay all suppliers, once a week. Those who do not have the ability to accept ACH will be paid with paper checks – but only twice a month.

- ACH debits used to pay all sales and use tax obligations with the states.

- All rush payments will be made with ACH. Special approval is required to issue a payment outside the normal payment cycle.

- Wire transfers will be used only in those rare instances where finality of payment is required, such as real estate transactions. Special approval is required.

- Issue travel cards to all travelers and instruct them to put everything possible on the card. Reimbursement of out-of-pocket expenses will be made via ACH to the account they designate. This can be different than the account used for payroll.

- Pay each vendor with one type of payment only.

Caveats

While it is ideal that you pay each supplier with only one type of payment, that is not always possible in the real world. For example, you might make a large purchase from a vendor slated to be paid by card and the dollar amount precludes the use of a card. There will also be the instances when the supplier in question does not take the payment type you offer.

Your payment strategy will evolve over time, as you gain experience and as new payment types emerge. Currently very few organizations are using Instant Payments.

That may change after the Feds make some changes in the next few years. So, stay alert.

Chapter 4
Fraud

New frauds translate into tactics and processes not previously used to protect against those new and innovative frauds. They mean organizations have to beef up their controls to ensure they don't fall for the latest scam.

Best Practice Strategies to Protect Against the Newer Technology-Based Frauds

The following are changes every organization should integrate into the accounts payable and payment functions. For if they don't, the result will not be pretty.

- **Fraud Protection Tactic #1**: Verify every single change of bank account request by calling a phone number you already have on file. Under no circumstance use a number provided in the email requesting the change. Some organizations take this one step further, calling the organizations main phone number and asking to be transferred to the party that can verify the change request is legitimate.

- **Fraud Protection Tactic #2**: Verify every single change of payment methodology request by calling a phone number you already have on file. More than one criminal has managed to figure out that an organization was paying using ACH and took advantage. They impersonated the supplier and tried to get the change made AND supply their own bank account number.

- **Fraud Protection Tactic #3**: Verify every single Rush wire transfer request from a high-level executive by either calling on the phone or actually going to their office. Too many email accounts have been compromised to make this step something that you can skip.

- **Fraud Protection Tactic #4**: Use a separate computer for online bank activity. This computer should not be used for email or surfing the Internet. This protects against an account takeover. This fraud doesn't happen frequently, but when it does, the results can be devastating. This protection tactic doesn't cost much and can save your organization millions.

- **Fraud Protection Tactic #5**: Internal controls should be strong and across the board, no exceptions. If there are weaknesses in your processes, your employees know where they are. Don't give them the opportunity to take advantage of this "insider" knowledge. Most internal fraud is committed by long-term trusted employees. Don't give them the opportunity!

- **Fraud Protection Tactic #6**: Identify suppliers who routinely send duplicate copies of invoices and closely scrutinize their invoices and payments. The problem of duplicate invoices has been growing over the last few years. While frequently suppliers who try this tactic are simply trying to get paid in a timely manner, a few bad apples have figured out this is a way to get a double payment. More than one copy of an invoice also creates a lot of extra work for the accounts payable staff – work that is definitely not a value-add.

- **Fraud Protection Tactic #7**: Whenever a duplicate payment slips through, investigate where the weakness was in your process that allowed this to happen – and fix it. If everything is working perfectly, a duplicate payment should not slip through. And, if it happens once the odds of it happening a second and third time are good. So, find the flaw and fix it.

- **Fraud Protection Tactic #8**: Bank reconciliations should be done on a daily basis to identify unauthorized ACH transactions. As soon as you find one, notify the bank. You only have a limited amount of time to refute these transactions and have the funds returned to your bank account. Even if you are outside the small "window of opportunity," still notify the bank. They may be able to get back some or all of the funds.

- **Fraud Protection Tactic #9**: Be alert for new frauds and adjust your processes to protect against them. Criminals are quite adept at finding ways around best practice processes. Sometimes all it takes is knowledge of the new fraud to protect your organization. Once the fraud mark knows about a new fraud and is then targeted, they immediately recognize it and don't fall for it.

- **Fraud Protection Tactic #10**: Educate everyone about new frauds as soon as you become aware of them. Knowledge is the silver bullet when it comes to fighting fraud. As soon as you become aware of the new fraud, share the information. Don't wait for the monthly staff meeting or when you have time to share, do it immediately. For every day you wait, is a window of opportunity for the criminals targeting your organization.

Check Fraud on the Rise: What You Can Do to Protect Yourself

Yes, it's on the rise! It's not just the new electronic fraud you need to worry about. Check fraud is skyrocketing and you won't believe what they are doing. Despite the declining use of checks in the United States, criminals have been increasingly targeting the mail to commit check fraud.

As you might imagine, COVID didn't help. While we've all been upping our defenses against the newest types of electronic payment frauds, criminals have gone back to basics, and they are getting more aggressive. As you'll see mentioned several times below, they are going so far as to steal checks right out of the blue mail collection boxes.

How bad is the problem? According to the USPS Office of Inspector General, Audit Report, between March 2020 and February 2021, there were 299,020 mail theft complaints, which was an increase of 161 percent compared with the same period a year earlier. Sadly, the trend appears to be continuing. Once again, check fraud is becoming big business.

How the Fraud is Committed

Criminals committing this type of fraud typically target the US mail in order to steal personal checks, business checks, tax refund checks, and checks related to government assistance programs. They don't discriminate. They'll take whatever checks they can get their hands on. That being said, there is one type of check they prefer to all others. The most valuable haul for the criminal is the business check Why?

There are several reasons why business checks are preferred. They include the fact that:

- It may take longer for the business to realize they have been defrauded

- There is a potential for a larger haul is there

- The recipient may not appreciate that the check was stolen for a longer period of time, giving the criminals more time to play their games before the account is closed.

As mentioned above, criminals are targeting mailboxes, both individual mail boxes as well as the USPS blue collection boxes. Once they get their hands on the checks, they use various techniques to alter items to get larger amounts of money as well as attempting to cash the check itself. Once the crook has the check, they also have the bank account number and transit and routing code to counterfeit additional items.

If the crooks find additional personal information when looking through your mail, they will exploit that as well. This data, along with the account information, is being sold on the dark web.

Protection Strategies

Since it is highly unlikely that paper checks are going to completely away, every person needs how to learn how to protect themselves and their organization. There are several ways to protect yourself. These include:

- Reduce the number of checks you issue as much as possible.

- Never put checks in a mailbox; take them to the post office for mailing. If the post office has those big blue collection boxes outside, do not use them. Take the checks into the post office for mailing.

- Use positive pay; or better payee name positive pay

- Reconcile your bank accounts on a daily basis

- Do not leave information about your bank accounts lying around where anyone can see it. Secure this information and shred any papers with it that are not needed.

- The minute you notice a problem, notify your bank

- If you are expecting a check payment, keep your eye on the mail. Bring the mail in as soon as you can. Don't leave it sitting all day, if you can possibly avoid it.

- If you are writing a check out by hand, fill in all blank spaces, even if it just means drawing a line through the space.

- As with other frauds, stay up to date on the latest developments, both of new frauds as well as the protection protocols.

In the US, paper checks remain a reality of life, albeit and increasingly smaller one.

Employing the most current protection protocols is a necessity, if you don't want to turn from a target into a victim.

Chapter 5
Evolving Best Practices

It goes without saying, that as business evolves, so do best practices – especially in accounts payable.

New Accounts Payable Best Practices Every Company Should Be Using

There's a number of reasons that best practices in accounts payable change; fraud protection and regulatory requirements being two key factors. The other big one, at least in the current environment, is the rapid expansion of technology. Not only is the price coming down, with options for every pocketbook, but most offerings are quite user-friendly. Let's take a look at three practices all best-practice organizations are incorporating into their procedures.

- **New Best Practice #1**: There are some new verifications every organization should use when setting up a new vendor in the master vendor file. The first is to verify the new vendor isn't on the US government's Specially Designated Nationalists (SDN) list. This is a list, updated several times a week, of every person, company and organization, US companies are not allowed to make payments to. Expect a number of false positives.

  The second recommended best practice, when setting up new vendors, is run the address of your new vendor against the addresses in your organization's HR file for payroll. The goal here is to ensure no employee is setting up a phantom vendor. There will occasionally be a false positive here, as well. So, research before an accusation is made. This won't catch every potential phantom vendor, but it's fairly easy to do and will catch a few of the ones who use their own address.

Some organizations take this process one step further also comparing TINs with social security numbers and bank account information. However, some HR departments will not let you do this due to state requirements and privacy concerns.

- **New Best Practice #2**: Verification of change of address for paper checks and change of bank account for electronic payments should be done before the change is made. This is to stop the exploding fraud criminals are using to target companies large and small.

The task should involve picking up the phone and either using a phone number already on hand or going to the company's main phone number and tracking down a billing, AR or Treasury person who can verify that the request is legitimate.

Ideally, the person confirming the request is legitimate is someone other than the person who sent the email or the letter asking for the change. The reason to talk to someone other than the requestor is to further guard against funny business in the supplier's organization.

Some complain that when they do this, they always receive a positive validation and that it wastes a lot of time. The reality is that most requests are legitimate. But, the one that is not can cost hundreds of thousands of dollars, if not more. So, please don't skip this step.

- **New Best Practice #3**: Best practices now include using IRS TIN Matching twice. The first time is as part of your vendor set up process. Any discrepancies should be resolved before the first payment is made. But then, at year end or in early January, run all potential 1099 information through IRS TIN Matching before you send out your 1099s.

Don't wait until the end of January do to this. TIN Matching may be overloaded at that point. But even more pressing, you may not have adequate time to get your mismatches resolved. After all, getting suppliers, especially those you are no longer doing business with, to respond in a timely manner, is difficult when you are asking about something they don't deem important.

Why might you want to do this? To identify any potential TIN/name mismatches before you issue the 1099s. This will save you getting B-Notices and having to deal with the IRS's onerous procedures for getting those mismatches resolved. It will also save you from potential fines and penalties and trying to get them abated. Why might there be mismatches, if you've already run the data through TIN Matching once before.

Organizations who have a change in circumstance that result in a changed 1099 reporting situation might forget to tell you. This might include a change in legal structure or a merger or acquisition. Some organizations take this one step further and run their entire vendor file through IRS TIN Matching once a year.

- **New Best Practice #4**: **W**hen purchasing an automation solution, make sure the one purchased as the ability to read invoices directly from email. By incorporating this feature, you will not have to annoy suppliers to change their existing processes, as they can continue to email invoices.

  If you don't have this feature in place, check with the service provider. They may have added this functionality sometime since your purchase and will show you how to use it. Anytime a supplier has to make a change, you can expect a lower adoption rate. With this feature in place the rate of usage for the solution should be much higher.

- **New Best Practice #5**: Receive as many invoices as possible by email. Many learned the importance of this when COVID first hit. This works whether you have the process automated or not, assuming you've followed the first best practice (if you purchased an automation solution. By encouraging vendors to send invoices electronically, companies can reduce the risk of errors and save on storage and handling costs.

Electronic receipt of invoices also makes the process of tracking and reconciling invoices easier. Still not convinced? Consider this. The US Post Office has indicated that everyone should expect snail mail to get even slower.

- **New Best Practice #6**: Stay on top of new frauds and the techniques and process changes needed to protect your organization against them. New frauds spread like wildfire, especially if criminals have a high success rate with their "new approach." This is one of those times when time really is of the essence. You don't have the luxury of waiting until you have some free time to catch up on all the latest fraud business intelligence. Once you become aware of a fraud, adjust your processes as needed so your organization doesn't fall victim to the latest scam.

- **New Best Practice #7**: Share fraud information with everyone: Fraud prevention is a team effort, and it's important for all employees to be aware of the latest threats and how to protect against them. By sharing information about fraud with everyone in the company, you can help ensure that everyone is vigilant in protecting against these types of attacks.

  Sometimes, just the knowledge of a particular scam is enough for people to realize that the particular request is fraudulent. Criminals have gotten quite good at targeting, not only high-level professionals but also mid-level staffers.

- **New Best Practice #8**: Make continuous learning a regular part of your routines. This should focus on all areas that touch the accounts payable and accounting functions. Don't overlook new technologies and the ever-expanding regulatory compliance issues. Books like this help, as do free resources like the AP Now ezine and the AP Now YouTube channel.

How many of these best practices are you already using? Are you going to implement the rest?

Chapter 6
Planning for the Future

The higher up you get on the proverbial corporate ladder, the more you need to be concerned about the issues management deems important.

Planning Your Career to Meet Management's Concerns, Both Short and Long Term

Step 1: The top concern of adoption of digital technologies that may require new skills or significant efforts to upskill/reskill existing employees falls right in line with the adoption of automation currently wafting through the function. As I write this, many are dealing with this very issue. It will be critical that all professionals continue to upskill to learn how to use the new technologies. It's not adequate to learn it once, but as updates become available, they need to be studied as well.

It should be noted that this includes apps such as Excel and whatever else your organization may be using. Please keep in mind that one of the biggest areas for opportunity related to the accounts payable function is related to the enormous amount of data that flows through the accounts payable systems.

By working with other departments and providing them the analytics they need, accounts payable will be able to help drive process improvements and cost savings.

When addressing the issue of upskilling, remember, management is also looking for those who can upskill their staffs. This is one of those soft skills rarely taught in schools.

Step 2: Stay current on all regulatory issues impacting the accounts payable function. This is a huge task, as the issues are numerous and the changes constant. While at first glance, this seems like a massive headache, it is actually a great opportunity.

All indications are that there will be more, rather than less, regulatory reporting required. And, ignoring those requirements is not a realistic option for companies looking to avoid trouble with organizations like the IRS, SEC and state taxing authorities.

Keep in mind that the Biden administration requested a huge increase in funding for the IRS and the IRS is looking to hire 200 additional attorneys. These actions speak volumes as to their intent to collect *ALL* the monies owed. And they need the help of those reporting, to ensure they have all the information they need to collect that money.

So, the unspoken area of opportunity in the coming years, will be around regulatory reporting. Those who are experts in these niche underserved areas should do very well.

Step 3: Be flexible; be willing to step outside your comfort zone and try new things. In order to be successful in the coming years, you will definitely need to do this. As new and disruptive technologies are introduced, make it a priority to learn about them and how they could improve your organization's operations.

Without a doubt, those who are successful in

the future will be those who are flexible and can adapt to new market conditions and technologies. Are you ready?

Preparing for the AP Department of Tomorrow: Your To-Do List

Looking into a crystal ball, no matter how cloudy it may be, there is one obvious prediction that can be made regarding accounts payable and that is this: There will be quite a bit of change impacting almost everything we do. When we look back five years from now at the way the accounts payable function is handled, it will be very different.

That's why, in this issue, we are focusing on the areas where we believe the most change will occur. Our mission is to make sure our readers have the tools they need to be successful in that accounts payable department of tomorrow, that brave new world where the accounts payable team is fully integrated into the accounting and finance function and where its members have a meaningful seat at the table.

The last year has been hard on many accounts payable operations, as well as the professionals who toil in them. Not only are they dealing with changes brought about by the necessity to go remote, there have been an onslaught of new frauds, IRS changes regarding 1099 reporting and now, new payment vehicles to deal with. And since time waits for no man or woman, the luxury of waiting until things slow down a bit is simply not in the cards.

To help our members, we've reviewed the issues and identified those areas where change is coming. We've included a check list to steps everyone should take to make sure they are prepared for the future. The temptation might be to skip some of the items, hoping you won't have to deal with them. But that is not a useful or realistic approach. Some will be easy to implement, like updating your travel policy for the new IRS mileage rate but others will require that you expand your horizons.

You'll notice that a few of the items recommend that you periodically review any changes that may have occurred in the business environment with regard to that issue. Keep track and note on your calendar so you don't forget to do the review.

You can use the checklist starting on the next page to make sure you address all the relevant issues as soon as is reasonably possible. You'll see a column to the left where you can mark off your progress, putting a check mark(√) when you've completed an item and an x, if it is an item you don't need to address. Of course, if you are really lucky, you'll already be doing some of these and you can cross them off the list.

1. Register for electronic filing of 1099s with the IRS, if you are not already done so. While the IRS has not indicated exactly when the threshold for electronic filing will drop, they expect you to immediately conform, and the drastic drop is expected in the very near future. Make sure your group is ready when that ball drops.

2. Review all your fraud controls to ensure you are integrating the latest fraud protection protocols, no matter how tedious some of them may be. This is especially important for your verification routines for email requests, as these frauds are especially vicious and are focused on the professionals working in accounts payable.

3. Review your payment process, especially if you are relying heavily on paper checks to make payments. There is a lot of change coming in this arena. Identify possible alternatives, that would work within your existing structure. This task should be repeated every 6-12 months given all the change.

4. Begin learning about real time payment options and determining which, if any, are reasonable for your operations. This will change over time, so a periodic review is probably called for. [See https://youtu.be/jKgmu-fye_E to hear Nacha's Rob Unger discuss the current state of Real Time Payments, including ACH.]

5. Begin learning about digital payment options and determining which, if any, are reasonable for your operations. This will change over time, so a periodic review is probably called for. [See https://youtu.be/I45FEn0vnI8 to listen to one manager who had to create a crypto payment process for her organization.]

6. Review your accounts payable policy and procedures manual to include processes for remote/hybrid work, assuming your organization plans to incorporate that type of work in the future. Pay special attention to the internal controls associated with this change.

7. Update your expense reimbursement policy for the new IRS mileage rate of 58.5 cents per mile. There is more information about this change in the Regulatory Update section of this publication.

8. Notify employees of new mileage rate, reminding them it is only for travel after January 1, 2022. A few crafty employees may try and put through November and December mileage at the new rate.

9. Create/update policy for reimbursing working from home expenses. Make sure this includes telling employees what will be reimbursed, what won't and how to pay for and report these items. [Expense report, p-card etc.] HR should be involved in reviewing

any changes to ensure it conforms to all legal and company policies.

10. If you haven't reviewed automation options for your accounts payable function in the last two years, this might be the time to at least view what several can do and get pricing. While not the solution for every accounts payable organization, professionals should be prepared to respond to management inquiries on this timely topic. This way, you are prepared to respond when the issue is raised. Sticking your head in the sand helps no one. And, those who are not satisfied with their current model, should investigate what's out there for there have been many changes and improvements.

About Mary Schaeffer

Mary Schaeffer, AP Now's Founder, has been creating content around the AP function for 20+ years. This material takes the form of a twice-a-week free ezine, a weekly podcast, a YouTube channel, a monthly newsletter, a variety of courses for accountants, and numerous webinars.

She is a member of Business Payments Coalition and Federal Reserve's Remittance Delivery Assessment Work Group, and Nacha's ACH Network Advisory Panel. Schaeffer has been named a Top AP Influencer for the last two years by the prestigious AP Association, a global organization headquartered in the UK.

She has a BS in Mathematics and an MBA in Finance. Before founding AP Now, she worked in corporate finance and treasury for three large multi-national companies.

Current Books by Mary Schaeffer

- 127 Best Practices for Accounts Payable (replaces 101 Best Practices for Accounts Payable)

- Fundamentals of Accounts Payable (second edition)

- Internal Controls in Accounts Payable

- An Accounts Payable Back-to-Work Action Plan (Post COVID)

About AP Now

AP Now is a membership organization, with both free and premium memberships. It provides the latest business intelligence related to the accounts payable and payment functions. Its members are professionals who work in, manage, or have responsibility for the accounts payable function, as well as the service providers who create and deliver products to that market.

Visit the AP Now website and sign up for its free twice a week ezine at:

www.ap-now.com

About AP Now YouTube Channel

Whether you are just getting started in accounts payable or are an experienced finance or accounting professional, with its 450+ videos, the AP Now YouTube channel has the latest business intelligence you need. At least one of the following playlists will meet your requirements:

- Accounts Payable Best Practices
- Changing Invoice Best Practices
- Accounts Payable Basics
- Accounts Payable Automation
- How Not to Make Mistakes in Accounts Payable
- Payments and Emerging Payment Issues
- Preparing for an Accounting/Accounts Payable Job Interview
- B2B Fraud Protection
- Working in Accounts Payable
- Master Vendor File Best Practices
- Duplicate Payment Avoidance

And more!

Access the AP Now YouTube channel at:

www.youtube.com/@APNow

Change in Accounts Payable

Change in Accounts Payable

Change in Accounts Payable

Change in Accounts Payable

Change in Accounts Payable

80